English Martyrs

Conor Carville is a poet and critic from Armagh, N. Ireland. His first collection, *Harm's Way*, was published by Dedalus Press. He lives in South London with his wife and daughter.

Also by Two Rivers Poets

David Attwooll, *The Sound Ladder* (2015)
Kate Behrens, *The Beholder* (2012)
Kate Behrens, *Man with Bombe Alaska* (2016)
Kate Behrens, *Penumbra* (2019)
Adrian Blamires & Peter Robinson (eds.), *The Arts of Peace* (2014)
David Cooke, *A Murmuration* (2015)
Terry Cree, *Fruit* (2014)
Claire Dyer, *Eleven Rooms* (2013)
Claire Dyer, *Interference Effects* (2016)
John Froy, *Sandpaper & Seahorses* (2018)
A. F. Harrold, *The Point of Inconvenience* (2013)
Maria Teresa Horta, *Point of Honour* translated by Lesley Saunders (2019)
Ian House, *Nothing's Lost* (2014)
Gill Learner, *Chill Factor* (2016)
Sue Leigh, *Chosen Hill* (2018)
Becci Louise, *Octopus Medicine* (2017)
Mairi MacInnes, *Amazing Memories of Childhood, etc.* (2016)
Steven Matthews, *On Magnetism* (2017)
Henri Michaux, *Storms under the Skin* translated by Jane Draycott (2017)
James Peake, *Reaction Time of Glass* (2019)
Tom Phillips, *Recreation Ground* (2012)
John Pilling & Peter Robinson (eds.), *The Rilke of Ruth Speirs:*
    New Poems, Duino Elegies, Sonnets to Orpheus & Others (2015)
Peter Robinson, *Foreigners, Drunks and Babies: Eleven Stories* (2013)
Peter Robinson, *The Constitutionals: A Fiction* (2019)
Lesley Saunders, *Cloud Camera* (2012)
Lesley Saunders, *Nominy-Dominy* (2018)
Jack Thacker, *Handling* (2018)
Susan Utting, *Fair's Fair* (2012)
Susan Utting, *Half the Human Race* (2017)
Jean Watkins, *Scrimshaw* (2013)
Jean Watkins, *Precarious Lives* (2018)

English Martyrs

Conor Carville

TWO
RIVERS
PRESS

First published in the UK in 2019 by Two Rivers Press
7 Denmark Road, Reading RG1 5PA.
www.tworiverspress.com

ISBN 978-1-909747-53-1

1 2 3 4 5 6 7 8 9

Two Rivers Press is represented in the UK by Inpress Ltd
and distributed by NBNi.

Cover design by Sally Castle
Cover image: Simon Marmion, *The Beast Acheron* from *The Visions of the Knight Tondal*.
The J. Paul Getty Museum, Los Angeles, Ms. 30, fol. 17
Text design by Nadja Guggi and typeset in Janson and Parisine

Printed and bound in Great Britain by Imprint Digital, Exeter

Acknowledgements

Thanks to the editors of *Prac Crit*, *Black Box Manifold*, *The High Window*
and *Axon*, where some of these poems first appeared.

I would also like to thank Peter Robinson, Steven Matthews, Shane Murphy
and Matthew Sperling for advice and support.

Contents

Bless

An Old Carved Doorknocker

The limewood hand that taps at the door
is much like my own, polished and cold,
for nothing whatever runs in the veins
that rise on the back of its flaking skin,
and the hinge that pinions it to the world
creaks and squeaks like no wrist should
as I feel the nub of the old amputation
where the index has broken away at the nail
and the white grain shows, thinking even so,
that if I am taking those fingers in hand
they're also taking mine: asking if anyone's
at home, knowing that this cannot be,
knocking and knocking again insistently.

Andromeda

Unaccountable Andromeda begins her rise
above the Great Salt Lake
and Smithson's *Spiral Jetty*:
for every star a glint of backfill,
for every mica-grain a star.

The powerful, glittering chains
hold all in place, place all on hold:
the sand and wave, surd and particle,
the scars on my skin, the memories I have,
weighty and invisible. 'All gone',

you say, looking up at your dad
and away from the miniature dish
of peas and carrots, cubed potatoes
and three individual crystals of salt.

Bog Thing

i.m. Seamus Heaney

I

Bales of printed matter,
combustible quires fresh
from the guillotine,
quartered tightly

in plastic twine,
then dumped
at the cross by the van
from the smoking city.

We watch it recede
a long time, until
the horizon's minus-sign
subtracts it finally.

I crook to lift the first
inky, recalcitrant stack,
straighten up to find
beneath it a smaller pack,

a ziplock bag
of imported comics:
intellectual *Marvel*;
spectacular *DC*.

II

As I came to see
the suppurating root
that hung at the heart
of things, I thought often

of the yellow-green
proboscis dangling
rigidly from the face,
how it swayed below

the powdery glow
of the two black sockets,
the neckless bulk
bathed, laved

in slime, slick with it,
seeming to bubble
as the first big spots of rain
intermittently plumped

the coarse pulp
to which my father's
back had turned,
benday dots

blending readily
with that thing
popularly referred to
as reality.

The Flip-Flop

Cast off at the door,
and kicked into touch,
coming to sit, beached
on the laminate floor

of this pastel hotel room
where a ceiling-fan
murmurs its rounds,
and the thing sits on

riding its own dim glow,
a plain base gripped
by a translucent strip
of resin. I'm wholly

given over to its insistent
stillness: a peasant's shoe,
but far from the boots,
rucked and truculent,

shucked off at the end
of the day to gape,
dog-eared, in Vincent's great,
hallucinatory painting.

No. It's slim as an insole,
clean as a *Polo*, with only
the faintest hint of a toe-tip
tainting the moulded foam

like a smudge in plush
or the painterly trace
of a *pentimento* face
beneath a shallow wash.

Geneva

At the edge of the primal lagoon for weeks,
I lean from lap-top to griddle
to lift the billycan lid, where a sweet-
smelling stew of rot and renewal
would normally be simmering but isn't,
given my guide's recent departure for
points unknown, though her ambition
one day was to visit Geneva
and the Large Hadron Collider.
No. This is a simple soup, a recipe
for the ages, if water can be said to be soup,
water and shell and a handful of bones,
scimitar-thin as fingernail parings
turning anti-clockwise on the water.

English Martyrs

After the throats descend from upstairs,
after their table-taps and creaks,
after the pong of Deep Heat
as the celebrant retires, sneakers
squeaking on the curly parquet,
the front of the chapel commences to sway,

to sway and little by little to dance
before my eyes, to clap, to hum;
and somebody up there must have a drum,
a djembe or keteh, is palming it once
or twice, unpacking a rhythm,
as the drone puckers up into song –

the song that is sung by the faithful departed
in their camps by the coast, the sonorous psalm,
the supplement that suspends and expands,
extraneous, yes, but somehow important;
the indexical link that sustains,
like the all-but-invisible wine-stain

the verger notes on the altar carpet, a stain
that might be ash but might be blood,
that another man would get down and scrub
but over which he has chosen
to brood, revolving it all
as he repoints the lectern and draws a veil

across the implausible past, a veil
that scales to the one in your
own life, lost on its line, a lime-spattered
sheet forgotten in a suntrap, some high-walled
courtyard rife with weeds and flowers,
its classical statues blurred to their nubs, martyrs

to the elements as these wooden statues are
to time, old lags, bolted to their shadows,
not a kick in the arse from the North Surrey Gallows,
where the barrelling juggernauts shudder
and slow before picking up once more,
gunning again for Dover and the globe.

Here's a thing: the evening crowd is global,
but all the deaths are Irish: O'Gorman,
Maloney, Shannon and Keogh. Some form
of correction there, the coursing flows
détourned, their pathways pitched
and tossed the way the networks switch

and twitch from moment to moment above
the Old Kent Road: its khat cafes
and Polski skleps and chip-unlocking offies;
its avenues of air-conditioned storage
for tulips and sushi, pharmaceuticals and art;
its start-ups and Pound Shops and its all-night nail bars.

Again the song starts up, again the dance,
again that lightning in the dome,
those faint synaptic flickers, images thrown
on painted clothes and eyes and hands
by a headlight's pass through mullioned glass,
the moving pentagrams of energy embossed

by all the power moving in and out of London
of an evening, currents that spin
the cities of the world within
their blazing orbitals: branded, brindled,
aligned in planetary rows ...
I hear them burn, and does my throat not open?

The Seminars III

More than that, the sunstruck biscuit tin
with Leopold's name on it,
currently floating
through Barney Kiernan's pub

in Little Britain Street
on page, let me check, page 345
of this foxed and fantailed copy
of *Ulysses*, the tin that in time

will quicken an earthquake,
the homely no-go zone
that's been torquing the room
in its fun-house interior, now begins

to pulse above the sodden sawdust
until, exiting the portal,
it becomes an 'incandescent
object of enormous proportions'

like a blip you'd see
lapsing from a radar screen
in Chelyabinsk, punters arching back
to scan the name on its spinning base,

which is *Jacobs* of Bishop Street,
home of the Fig Roll and the Mikado,
bought out by Danone
and subsequently acquired by Kraft,

as it locks a tractor beam on Bloom,
warming, shaking him a little,
as an infant might shake a bottle of pop
to calibrate the turbulence within.

The Icons of Leningrad

Their winter skies are thronged with holes
in circles and outlines, parallel arcs,
nail-marks streaking off towards heaven
and shorter bursts, the trail of dots
that ends an unfinished sentence ...
Or tracer fire above a city, the bullets
cast from salvage melted down:
statues; railings; finally, a last resort,
the metal rims and torcs and discs
given up by icons, that hard-faced,
redoubtable virgin, this peasant saint
who seems to think the patch of teak
vacant at his head, unvarnished ground
inside the missing halo's disappearance.

Red Sails in the Sunset

The charity shop is full of terrible paintings,
every one of them the same: the sun
going down on a lone silhouette, a yacht
interrupting a strangely placed horizon.

It's a funny old world. *Red Sails in the Sunset*
is a song by Jimmy Kennedy, of *Hokey Cokey* fame.
Who also wrote: *The Teddy Bear's Picnic*
and *It's Istanbul (not Constantinople)*.

Each and every figure has its back turned,
whether for reason of art, or lack of skill
or some deep, deep distress I cannot tell. All
in black, they might well be wearing wet suits.

I ask you. The Hokey Cokey was a dance
performed by Canadian miners. *The Teddy Bear's
Picnic* was J. G. Ballard's favourite song.
Constantinople is another name for Istanbul.

Lurid, putrid, pooling light. Ropey contours
swirling as wave echoes coast echoes cloudscape.
And there's no going back now. No escape,
the sails swing wide to leeward, the clusters

of canvas peak sharply, silently,
under a sun dully shining without rays.
Red sails in the sunset, way out at sea.
The figure with its back to you is me.

Apelles

Your answer to the question of the sky
was in the negative. Impressed no end,
I looked beyond the flitches of your hair –
the fronds, the swathes – to see a brace
of small, bumpy clouds, widely spaced
and coloured *blue*, while the white page
kept its counsel high above the playground
and the problem of the rotor-blade
was skewered by a minus sign as thin
as the one Apelles, dropping in to find
him out, drew beside Protogenes's work,
where it remained until destroyed by fire
in the seventh year of the common era.

Poem for Delia Derbyshire

First silence, then clanking and soon
a pattern emerges, though ponderous with it,
like the analogue tape of a clutch of skittles
hitting the deck of a bowling emporium

you recorded off the cuff near Shepherd's Bush,
slowed to a lugubrious soup, then spliced
and looped till satisfied, threading it past the heads
with your unpalsied hand, and not for any old rubbish,

but the dark impresario's posthumous opus, missing
or never produced, where a balding man,
bespectacled, somewhere in that narrow zone
where Eric Morecambe meets Philip Larkin,

looks up from his occult researches to sweep
somnambulant and narcotized, as far
as the window before the camera cuts, reversing
to an exterior shot of his cornea steeped

in the ink of its ruptured pupil, a primordial *Quink*
that settles to reveal the bone-clad wagon,
its wicker of ribs, its thigh-yoke and bone-stanchion,
its skeletal horses stooping their beaks to drink.

Hanatarashi

While Yamantaka Eye of *Boredoms*
was driving that canary-yellow backhoe
right through the wall and onto the stage
of some dive in the back-end of Osaka
and was forcibly detained before he could throw
a Molotov cocktail into the mosh-pit,
my younger self was pinching the intractable tip
of an oyster-grey candle-style light-bulb, easing it in
to the point where it flashed into being,
slightly singing the pad of my thumb
and hurling me onto the bed where the last thing
I heard was the camouflaged palanquins drawing up
and maidens ducking out to greet them
with gifts of rats and frogs and burning arrows.

The Seminars X

I who hung out with Conrad and Marlowe
in a cinder-block lock-up
on the Isle of Dogs and who,
in the back-room of a louche bistro

somewhere in the Fifth, was there
when Beckett met Eliot and Burroughs:
three perfect Victorian gents, identikit
in Pringle and polyester, though Bill

wore a Stetson and was quite possibly
packing, and Sam had the edge
with his dark blue corrective shades
and paper tube of tipped cheroots.

The three of them sat across the table
so quiet and old-school polite
that Sontag and Ginsberg
had to deliver the goods

conversation-wise
(not a problem
for that pair of windbags),
but what amazed me most

was the way El Hombre Invisible
left the room with no-one the wiser,
how Eliot seemed to be wearing
a hint of expensive foundation

that gave his face a greenish tinge,
how they bonded over golf:
cleeks and jiggers,
dormies, the merits

of the mashie nib,
the way that Beckett stood
at midnight with a furled umbrella
to demonstrate the Vardon grip.

The Brides of Crossrail

Last night, on my clapped-out laptop,
I watched an image slowly germinate
deep in the darkened matrix
of the Extremely Large European Telescope.
It wobbled and stopped, then wobbled again
in the way the quartz confetti of a TWOC
on the kerbstone of our cul-de-sac
must stop and wobble when
Ada Lovelace, Phyllis Pearsall,
or one other of the Brides of Crossrail
turns over to begin the daily grind,
and I find myself alive
to the veil of spoil that flutters before her,
the skirt of sparks that comes in her train.

The Bunnysuit

Acephalos rabbit, man-headed coney,
smoking in the hidden grove,
when you go home, kick back, disrobe,
what is it that is scraped away

to hum on the floor, grubby and tufted,
warm still, dry-clean only?
If the weight of the average human
soul is roughly the same

as that of an empty bunny suit,
this one's a doozy, slashed
at the throat, the head hanging back,
the silken innards fully exposed

as another miniature goes down,
and the fête continues
to be sponsored by
a firm of local estate agents.

Enumerate the holes: beneath the arms,
beside the groin, behind the lappy lugs –
six organs of admittance –
for it gets hot in there, and dark,

the panting loud inside your head,
and you can smell your body as it burns
what you have offered it: cupcakes
and hard liquor; a sausage on a stick.

The Ballad of R. D. Laing

Between the skull in Connemara
       and the one beneath the skin
lies the album sleeve aglimmer
       in the bargain-columbarium
of a charity shop in Banglatown,
       Banglatown or Stepney,
the skull that glows, all unbeknown
       where poetry and psychiatry
shacked up for a time, their Magic-Eye
       polarities in strobing flux:
as duck scuppers bunny,
       so bunny morphs to duck.

I tug it from its berth in the depths,
       twig as the legend appears
above the image: *Life before Death*,
       in a 70s font, some weird
Bodoni or Didi, underneath it your
       proto-photoshopped
head, a double exposure of spirit
       and bone, empty sockets
skilfully superimposed
       on greyscale skin
like two osculated snow-globes
       pimped to a cultic bonce.

Slanting the cover I peer again
       at the funny head, follow
each orbit's rim to the deskilled join
       where sinkhole
eyes are counter-sunk to throw
       ripples of flesh through
a mandarin's forehead. Below
       are swags of adipose

that fall away into the shadows
            massing inside the coombe
of your scooped-out brain-bowl
            bereft of lobe, gunk-lubed.

The innermost sleeve slides out
            okay but the disc is unfeasibly
scundered, a crockery of claw-
            marks and keratotic lesions
with maximum haggle points; also
            there's the clammy
tang of some kind of decomposing
            linctus released,
infusing swaying nostril groves
            with memories of my Father's
clothes at breakfast, home
            unspeaking from Special Care.

I see cut-ups and duct-tape, Krapp
            at his tape-deck
manipulation. Delia spooling a loop
            while Burroughs prospects
along the bloody seam open
            on his desk between
two columns, the self-same
            broken line stealing
along the hominoid cranium's
            basal ridge where
the reptile brain teeters on
            the haunch of my shoulder.

I think of the golden portal-plates
            of Tutankhamun's death-mask,
the infinite reticence of its face
            weighty as a star impressed
on the laminated library book I scored
            in a memorable foray
deep into the Paranormal
            aisle while Granny was away

hoking and execrating in Needle-
         Craft. Also in that haul
the spin-off paperback from *Arthur C Clarke's*
         Mysterious Worlds.

Its cover's crystal Aztec skull
         ascends now like a new-born
planet above the white
         horizon of my brain
as I assume the position and someone
         removes my head, setting
it down on the floor, its little gown
         of polyps notwithstanding,
from where it can watch and laugh
         and sing this air
as the skull of R. D. Laing
         bestirs itself and is prepared.

The album-cover skull extrudes. By degrees
         it eases up with
mycological growth, it creaks
         against the image of itself,
becoming first a bas-relief and then
         a peaky death-mask
prized from its station
         to stand in the round, fully plastic
at last and held up solemnly
         above the stiff upstanding
void of my neck, onto which it's carefully
         threaded: turning, turning…

…turned and turned like the tricky
         anti-tamper cap that seals
your bottle of tricylics:
         Clozapine, Aripiprizole,
or your little jar of pineal
         pills, smiley obols, reuptake
prophylactics, screwed tight until
         it comes right with a click,

and the eyes that aren't mine
      light up to look round
to catch my own bright eyes
      that hesitate, cast themselves down.

The eye cast down, the cast in the eye
      of a shrunken head
in The Museum of Mankind.
      The bright bone shelled
from such a skin, clean as a conker,
      seat of the soul. The whole
kit and caboodle reduced
      to a sponge on the spear
of the spine: a totemkopf, hopped up
      on dopamine; the sallow rebel,
spiked on a pole above the portcullis,
      halfway to becoming a skull.

Poem for Karou Abe

Just as against the bone-sundering waters
of the Shindo falls, or the Nachi or Fukuroda,
the itinerant flautists of the Shogunate
would pit their plaintive shrieks, even so
on weekday mornings Tokyo's enormous roar
receives the semaphored entreaties
of saxophone, trumpet and electric guitar
from the mummy's boys that line the Sumida.
As we crossed the stinking river I asked: *Master,*
how is it they get down there? He replied
by standing his flight-case on its side
and unpicking the clasps. It opened like a door
into Stuka screams and Superfortress thunder,
a thousand banshees in formation over Chiba.

After Jeff Wall's After *'Spring Snow'*

For Peter Robinson

Someone has come between you
and me and the big picture: the Japanese girl
who turns away from it all

and endeavours to shut
the door of her cab, the hack
in which she was hoping to flee

the extinction event,
the singularity of light
that sizzles on the smoking nitrate.

Not a cab.
A Model T Ford. Its period interior
cooked up in Jeff Wall's Vancouver,

where the pilotless ships
from Kowloon and Kobe
economize by never stopping,

slowing instead to a shuddering throb
while the great containers
levitate, rising up of their own accord

like Warhol's silver balloons,
filling the air as if
they were filled with air

instead of widgets
and mobility scooters,
frying pans and superconductors,

as if they were leveraged
by nothing at all, or something
thin as the hiss that leaks

from the security guard's discreet earpiece
as he comes between you and me
and the big picture.

The Seminars VIII

It's with Alain, Judith and Slavoj
I should be, on a video link,
rampant on the digital field, waving
my beard and plucking my armpits

on *Skype*, live and direct from Saas Fee.
Saas Fee! Uniquely dynamic,
creative, crammed with encounters.
And the money: don't get me started.

With Giorgio and Avital
and Antony Gormley, that should be me,
making interventions from the back
in a pincer movement with Alenka Zupancic.

For I am box office and I demand
top dollar, that and a personal chalet
high above the snow-line, Zen-like
in its lack of personal comfort,

but rich with creative encounters.
Yes, I will immanentize the eschaton
from a lair in Saas Fee, the Swiss resort
immortalized by George and Andrew

in the video for *Last Christmas*.
Sass Fee, I give you my heart,
for like you, I am uniquely dynamic: I,
who once had a drink with Andrew O'Hagan.

Camouflage

Across the planet things are disappearing,
scattered into trees and cones and fields,
into cylinders, cubes and waves, undermined
or broken down, their outlines smeary
like the mud-lashed tender on Raspail
that so intrigued Picasso who, though war
had come, had not seen camouflage before.
We did that was what he said to Stein.

A white cross on white sky, I climb
into the morning's minimal ontology
allowing the weave of the grid to hold me
high above the earth, where those in the know
are bivouacked in a stripe on the haunch
of an incandescent tiger by Rousseau.

The Birthday Party

The Disney balloon is attached to my head
by dint of static from a recent buzz-cut.
It is Beauty I believe, one of many princesses

at this party.
      The three-year-old hordes
ignore the grapes and seeds, the novelty
divots of carrot and banana,

but cavort about the cheesy strings
like extremophiles round the belching vents
that line the Mariana Trench.

Something like that.
                I find I have nothing to say
to the software developer from JP Morgan
concerned that his aesthetic life

is at the mercy of the bank's conservatism
in design matters.
      I nod my head. Beauty
bobs gently, shudders, squeaks softly

against the airing cupboard, where,
concealed inside a hessian Bag-for-Life,
lies the pearly grey of a christening robe
cut out from the wartime wedding dress
that was stitched from a bolt of parachute silk
that was torn from an elm in '43.

The chute came down in Carrick-on-Shannon.
The tree fell prey to the Dutch disease.
The silk was synthesized by IG Farben.

The Pitbull

'Gucci!' A shout in the street. I peek sideways
through the window, down to the gallery's
cobbled courtyard where men in paper suits

are unloading Antony Gormley. Not Antony Gormley
himself, but *Antony Gormley*, the exhibition.
Which is composed of replicas of Antony Gormley.

Can't source the voice. Its echo screwing back and up
above the steamy, rattling kitchens: 'Gucci! Gucci!',
ringing out above the bodies where they lie, pent

in metal caskets, shorn and swathed, bedded
down in memory foam, or prone already, toe-tagged
on the big white sheets. Two-hundred grand a pop.

Then it canters into view: the pink-eyed mutt,
the one-eyed dog, muscling in, prancing across, the meshed
and rippling skin carelessly stretched across flesh

and bone, a flexing sleeve of silk and miniver,
as if the pelt were gathered up and back
by the tight-fisted stump of the top-knotted tail,

as if that tense little spindle were torquing the eyes,
the empty one and the full, slanting them back
along the close-knit flanks of the jaw-bone,

as if a skanky invisible bit were curling back
the corners of the mouth, the black lips peeled
to reveal the flecked and moistened carnadine.

Gucci out of Oxide out of Cronus out of Lexus,
Fatal out of Rocky out of Pluto out of Loco,
Saorsie out of Sushi out of Kipling out of Tlaloc.

I am thinking of Antony Gormley, shrink-wrapped
in cling-film, a shivering cellophane mummy,
hearing the shuck and the slap of the smoking plaster

that will dry in an hour to a flaking stiff, a body bag
for a moment of time, a posture, a gesture,
feeling the breeze in the brieze-block hangar

as the plaster cast is broken open, carefully
prized away from his body, as shells are prized away
from the flesh of the crabs in the restaurant below me,

shell after shell, crab after crab, hour after hour,
then scuttled in a yellow bucket, the pearl-grey
of their insides lined with fronds and flitters of flesh.

Gucci out of Nibhaz out of Nomos out of Baal,
Bezek out of Rémy out of Kukri out of Yves,
Yoda out of Scud out of Kishi out of Igloo.

'Gucci! Gucci!' Slower now. Curious. Trotting squatly
and diagonally down towards the blue-chip
statues, the gallery hands oblivious, faces blurred

by the steam of their breath: 'Gucci! Gooch!', his loose metallic
leash atrail: it coils, uncoils, shimmies, undulates
its armour-plated tinkle quietly over ice-cold cobbles.

Cobbles that are swelling from the earth
like the sculpted pates of an underground troop
of ancient sculptures by Antony Gormley,

buried long ago to guard the primal Father's stash,
of gem-bedizened skulls and crystal Bugattis
and further sculptures by Antony Gormley: 'Gucci! Gucci!'

Gucci out of Roxy out of Tupac out of Sasha.
Gucci out of Guisarme out of Kairos and Atilla.
Gucci out of Axel out of Hermes and Kenosis.

The statues lie on in the cobbled yard, bodies of men,
laid out on the freezing ground, grey-blue, blue-
black, tenderly mortised where shoulder meets neck,

as if smeared there with some kind of shadow-cack,
as if the terrible joins were caulked with darkness,
for this is the hour in which the streets fill up with darkness,

lapping just below the limen, sipping at the glassy welts
of the seams that suture the segments of each torso,
the coppery psoriasis on flanks and forearms,

the gelid heads, the stoppered ears, the thumbed-out eyes,
the mouths no more than a shallow dinge, the arms
stitched closely to their sides. Gucci. Gucci. Gucci.

A working dog, lurker on stairwells, barker
in culverts, weaponized with a bolt-cutter's
nick to the arse then lobbed at a doorman's face, or

hung to strengthen jaws by jaws alone, high
on the slender trunks of saplings newly planted
in the dusty park, throbbing white grenade

suspended by its pin, the tree bent almost to the
ground, the dog latched on to be catapulted up-
wards, thrashing and whirling the while,

a fanged gyre stripping the bark, splintering
the branch, to drop only when the wood cracks
and the tree collapses broken-backed. Gucci! Gucci!

Gucci out of Attis out of Calvin out of Glock,
Kapo out of Custer out of Tekko out of Frigg,
Louis out of Mithras out of Ralph and Bec de Corbin.

I'm as heavy as Antony Gormley encased in a shell-suit
of mud, for the moment I go to open my mouth it is filled
with clay and scrim. I'm heavy as a golden butt-plug

in the freezing gloom of a Pharaoh's tomb
above a heaving restaurant in Bermondsey. 'Gucci!
Gucci!' Light-headed, half-lit from the first drink

in months but gravid, too heavy for this world, the floor
bowing beneath me, its Victorian boards, as the warmth
leaks away leaving only the statues and Gucci and me.

They've seen him now, the techs, stepped back in unison
like some kind of boyband, as he sniffs the crotch
of the outermost statue, getting warm, ignoring his minder,

'Gooch! Gucci!', who has booted round the corner and
stopped to assess the scene: the techs, the rigid bodies
on the cobbles, the dog, 'Gucci mate!', warm, the dog who nuzzles

the head now, warmer, his hot dog-breath condensing
on the iron neck, 'Gooch, Gucci!' his trembling belly
warming the carbonized lug as I return to life myself, 'Gucci!

Gucci!' warm enough to return, to turn away, as Gucci turns away,
cocking a leg, warm, warmer, spiralling back downstairs
to the warmth, the glow, the light, 'Gooch! Gucci!', warm,

warmer, the yellow glow, the light of the brands, the logos,
the glow, Gucci, the steaming plates, warm, warmer, 'Gooch!
Gucci!', the sparkle, the light, the glowing flesh, back by your

side, warm, warmer, the flitters, the fronds, Gooch, Gucci,
the wine, the warmth, the glow in my throat, Gucci, Gooch,
warm, warmer, back by your side, finally safe, the steam,

the snow, the yellow glow, finally sure, Gooch, Gucci, warm,
warmer, back by your side, the steam the glow the yellow snow,
Gucci, Gucci, warm, warmer, finally sure, finally safe, warm,

warmer, safe in the knowledge, back by your side, warm, warmest,
Gooch, Gucci, back by your side, safe in the knowledge
that somewhere a pitbull is pissing on Antony Gormley's head.

Cinema

1. 2001: A Space Odyssey

In this way one thing becomes another:
the intelligent craft, intricate
against the sumptuous décor of the cosmos,
a slim harmonica in its satin-lined box,
begins to tilt around its axis,
but in doing so falls out of the frame
and the next thing you know
there's a yellow bone in the sky.

Or was it not the other way round?
That's for you to say. I was asleep
in the smallest cinema in London,
floating gently in the dark, the light
of my daughter's unborn face
reflected on the surface of my visor.

2. Solaris

It wasn't a movie, you said, much later,
speaking of the three-hour film
to which I'd begged you to come,
something about a beautiful, menacing planet
that took on the dreams of those
who fell into orbit around it. I had pleaded.

Importuned. Though I'd be the one to fall
asleep as soon as we got there,
even before the trailers began: comatose,
a neomort, dead to the world
that trembled on the screen
of the sepulchral craft, a shivering membrane,
thinly stretched, and rife with storms and tides.

The Seminars XV

The weather today is brought to you
by *Powergen*, the sky today
is brought to you by Habakkuk, the stars
tonight are brought to you by *Pokémon*.

Your class today is brought to you
By *South-West Trains*, the time
it took was brought to you
by the letter K and the number 5

Number 5 and the letter K
Were brought to you by *Glaxo Kline*,
Glaxo Kline by Averroes, by Zollikon,
by the Diddymen and Gordon Gumma.

Your moods today were brought to you
By total football, *Xenidate*, your sex today
Was brought to you by
Harry Potter and the Problem of Evil.

The extracts on your hand-out
are sponsored line-by-line
by the following establishments:
Chicken Express, Perfect Chicken,

Chicken Hong-Kong, Chicken Ding-Dong,
Chicken-in-a-Bap, Chicken-on-a-Rope,
Manicure chicken, Pedicure Chicken,
Vernacular Chicken. Chicken Oedipus.

The turning ground beneath your feet
was brought to you by glaciation,
soil erosion, time frottage,
apocalyptic bukakke.

The interminable description
of Gabriel's whitey at the end of 'The Dead',
was brought to you by the Shining Path,
By Origen, by Zebedee and Fanny Craddock,

by the cedar tree whose heaviest branches
Sweep Front Quad
with their long heavy lashes. Listen.
They make the sound of waves and ashes.

Bless

1. Regal

Wimbledon, shit ... I'm still only in Wimbledon,
and here's you seated on the sofa growing
stronger by the second. Nowadays
the slice-and-dice of rotors overhead betokens

not the smoking-out of a crack-house, or a Wessex
fossicking its way across the drumlins,
but the Bells or Sikorskis that bring
oligarchs to Chelsea in the Spring. *Bless.*

Bless them all: Camberwell and Peckham Road.
The South London Press and its small-
ads for jumble. A black *Gola* hold-all
dispatched one October from Aldergrove,

accompanied by its callow minder, me:
the hold-all that held all: a change of clothes,
a duty-free carton of *Embassy Regal*,
and my extensive travelling library

of one book, a 21st present that July:
the orange-spined, white covered edition
of Gunter Grass's *The Tin Drum*,
largely unread, even today.

'You mean to say, you were telling me lies?'
Yes. 'You mean to say you never read those books.'
No. 'All those books you save on your phone?'
I have never opened a book in my life.

2. The Ward

The perfectly circular floor-length column
of plastic curtains around the bed
where my Father has fallen asleep
has no centre. Its circumference passes
through every point in the universe.

3. Playscape

This little picture is your logo Daddy,
the way you look to others. See.
Tap it. What would you like to be?
You can choose to be a girl or a boy'.

I would like to be a girl, small
and brave and unimpressed,
with a little tin drum at her belly,
a voice that can shatter glass.

'Done. Now these guys are the mini-beasts,
There's a bunch of them, right? Here
is one. Tomsk. He's a Womble, yeah? And another.
Now start walking. Keep your eyes on your mobile'.

I cannot rub from my eye the strangeness
I get from this shattered screen,
the splinter in my eye
that magnifies the hoary grass.

'Ohhh-kaaaay... Now this is my Avi. Look
her name is Emily, she collects things
to help you against the old King
who can't believe he's dead. Well? What do you think?'

I think I am in a strange land,
sitting by the fire, feeling its glow,
wearing a winter cloak,
with a smartphone in my hand.

4. Never Get out of the Boat

Morning in the social factory.
Writer, broadcaster and male comedian
Jasper McGoombay has joined us on the sofa
to talk about fatherhood, his guff underwritten

by incoming news on a scarlet ribbon:
the Northern Line is suspended;
London Bridge is closed; another head
has been found on Wimbledon Common.

I'm watching telly with no sound, the laptop
propped, precarious on the sofa's arm,
ladling gloop into our first-born.
Rhubarb and Custard. Noggin the Nog.

Bless. I lost my head thirty years ago.
Jasper witters on in dumb-show,
as the sofa starts to shudder and sway, its go-
away-green offset with a camouflage throw,

a chalky choker of tyres lashed to its arms.
As if this were a sloop on the Mekong.
As if this were a raft on a branch of the Amazon.
We'll build a bigger boat when we get to the ocean.

5. Spital

Get this. Last night I was awakened by an echo through my
    chamber,
a peal or a chime, more chime than peal, less chime than the
    Ping!
of a monitor's sonic signature, the kind of a note you hear when
    a pang
is under surveillance, a pang or twinge, that class of a beep you
    encounter

in an ICU, where the veiled and scrutinized creature lies, both
    dead and alive,
dead to the world but alive, his vital signs outsourced, *Ping!*,
    subsisting
on credit, *Ker-Ching*! His brain-stem dried to a spongiform
    chalk and the brain
a white, sacrificial coral, beached in the comatose dark, the syn-

apatic pathways alkaline and powdered, dusty as the Martian
    canals
though the body jogs on, *Ding-Dong*, a set of values on a screen,
    a data-bleed,
a risk prediction triggered from an off-shore platform, all
    studded with feeds
and acanthus leaves, all schooled and wreathed in loop-
    the-loops, the hula-hoops

of transparent tubes, drips and traps and lianas, catheters,
    peacock feathers,
stents and shunts and libations, *Slurp*, the flexible grails of
    pumps and gates
through which devolve the hormones that flow, *Hi-ho! Hi-ho!*
    along the networks
and branches and nodes, along the pathways that flow,
    the routers that sow

the gene that codes for death, and the gene that codes for grace,
the gene that codes for love, and the gene that codes for art
the gene that codes for Soma, and the gene that codes for Sarx.
The gene that codes for dream. The gene that codes for gene.

6. The Watchtower

No school today, apparently, so we drift
to the Common, and while she plays, I skirmish
with the gleaming testudo of mothers
in identikit black inflatable puffas

and blinding riding boots, circled prams
the size and weight of armoured cars.
I dredge my phone and search for the heart
beneath the playground's USP, an alarming

wood and thermoplastic watchtower
Ting! Its peaked roof and a palisade,
its searchlight, sniper loop and slide,
the ivy-woven netting that throws

a grid upon the earth's weird glow,
the earth that is neither round nor flat,
the dark blue earth turning violet
in the shade of the willows.

At four the sun is a parachute flare
warily sinking behind the tower,
weak as a tea-light on the river
at da Lung, as a nixie on the Neckar.

The muddy chute-mouth darkens,
but the kids play on, burning the fats.
A cloud you've seen before above the hut:
blue-veined, the back of your hand.

7. Ping

The little girl has found a thing
in my mobile phone, it is round, like a planet.
Oval. She picks it up, pops it in the digital basket,
and before you know it we're at the watchtower. *Ping.*

Bagpuss O Bagpuss O fat furry Catpuss. We stand,
the two of us, and crane up at the hut, high in the air
and blitzed with tags, *Ping,* some of which begin to stir:
the mice on the mouse organ. Gabriel the toad.

Hastily, none too daintily, she puts the object down,
as the pearl-grey knitting-needle whiskers clack
into view above us, *Ping,* then down the slide it backs,
Ping, Ding, Ting, emerging from the tunnel-mouth

arse-about-face, its hackles fizzing static, as if spiked
with sugared water, standing on end like a frightwig
so it seems to grow in size, the colour changing too, *Ping.*
Pink and white transformed in hue to scarlet and black.

Above the head a think-bubble appears, in it is Emily's thing.
A small, red rubber heart, all dusty with dust. Also a farty
little dog. Small and white. A hand appears to be holding the heart.
Out to the dog. More paw than hand. All is red and black and white.
    Ping.

The dog takes the heart in its mouth, gently, gently. As it does,
I see a heart no longer but rather a mummified head.
I look for the thing that Emily found, the original thing.
    Disappeared.
Was it a head? *Ping.* Was it a heart? *Ding.* O fat furry catpuss.

8. Memorex

I'll be plumbed in tubal purgatory, dunked
in the memorex churn of retro kids' TV,
or a public information flick where
a Zurbaran ghoul in a sack-cloth hoodie

beckons you towards a septic tank,
when some class of a non-space kicks in:
a chilly institutional scene, keyed to a greyish colour
unknown to Farrow & Ball. Let's call it *Adorno's Breath*.

The pulsing time-stamp says its now,
[03.35 AM], but otherwise the scene preserves
the spectral replicant candour
of the totally generic: strip-lit narrow

rafts or pallets tightly packed
along a corridor of polished concrete,
off which lie modular hangars stacked
with forms, some naked, some shrouded.

Normal programming resumes
with early 80s Eastern European animation:
Once Upon a Dog, *A Kitten named Woof*,
Lie Dream of the Plasticine Crow.

But not before the drone ascends to a bird's-eye,
and something glossily fat and black
beetles up the screen. A canteen trolley?
A cleaning lady? No. A ... a mobility scooter.

9. Bio

He stored his heart in a pint-pot of formaldehyde
where it bleached for years to a flaking bulb, a puffa fish
on a shelf in his man-shed, sequestered between the brew kit
and the decommissioned naggin of *Paraquat*, a portable shrine

He'd exhibit of an evening, declaring: 'This is the soft star,
the eternal diagram, that doubles my body'. *O do us a favour,*
we answered back, *Nobody believes in that kind of cack any more.*
Kantorowicz? The old ways are dead, these days it's all about the Walter

Benjamins, man, it's all about the Karl Schmitts and Giorgio
  Agambens.
Then it disappeared, stolen by a Womble, and he changed
overnight: some bright and invisible substance flowed away and,
  purged,
abstracted, he lightened, like a balloon animal, like a poodle by
  Koons.

That same night the stars fell down to earth and lodged in bodies,
  first
Alpha Ceti did, then Beta, then another and another,
  so the constellations
latched onto the turning globe, pinhole by pinhole, their sparks
  hived
in the crook of an arm, or entering an ankle Milton-style
  as the earthly

planetarium and the cosmos were elided, like two elasticated sides
of an endless complex surface, through which runs the substance
  of this life:
human resources, cosmic gases, money, electrical forces,
  high-frequency
currents, all coursing undimmed in the shape of a whale,
  a Leviathan
that throbs and moans its way through our civil death, floating in

        the dim
blue fluorescent anti-injecting light of the void, pierced
    by the light-show
of the legions of wounds that seed its flukes and fleck its bony
    prow,
by the great bar-code of infernal light that filters intermittently

through its mouth-grille, behind which you can see us,
    the multitude
of homunculi, our massed backs turned to you, gazing raptly and
    intent
at some invisible vanishing point, the locus at which the great
    cetacean's
stomach wall is rent and furled, hooked back by a hand to one
    side,

like the shuddery rubberized flap of an old-school psych-ward
    doorway,
through which can be seen another a hand, a hand with a wound
    on its back,
floating, disembodied, the hand of a ghost, the ghost
    in the whale, its
out-stretched finger not quite touching the crowned heart's
    pulsing ruby.

10. Paraclete

What kind of thing is a symbolic Daddy?
Only I have to do a symbolic tomorrow.
The drawing I made of us all at the tower.
Is that a symbolic? With Grandad? On his machine?

Remember the noise in the chimney draft,
that was echoed in turn by another whistle?
That night his small mechanical raft
ran aground against the beautiful crystal.

Meh. I can't even remember doing him. Show
me again? He must have landed from that helicopter,
the shadow behind him might be his para-
thingy. *Paraclete.* What's that he's holding?

He has taken the bone-handled pen-knife
from my Adventure Kit, *and is peeling*
His daily apple, carefully carving slice after slice,
salting them with sugar, eating them from the blade.

I like the way I have done the sky.
Blue clouds in white air. That you are watching me,
not your mobile. I like mummy. The heart between
us floating. If it was nowadays, I'd do it differently.

I want to sleep on the ceiling of your picture,
near the very top of the tower,
where the sky is drawn the wrong way round.
I want to sleep on your little blue cloud.

11. The Shepherd of Being

I'm alone again, the early hours. The PC fades
again to grey, again the pallet-rafts
resolve, the corridor is unconcealed,
though now the camera lingers, wafts

down to the door of a catering lift
from which the tip of a scooter-
prow juts, a vacant face
masked it seems with masking tape.

The Shepherd of Being.
The Psychiatric Nurse of Being.
The Mushroom-picker of Being.
The Tyre-plant Operative of Being.

After the scooter's thrum has dwindled
there come grunts, hootings,
the claw-ticks of walkers,
loping, unspeaking, sniffing the air.

Four squat hairy shadows,
four fat furry interlopers; the smell,
its frieze of polymers and glue,
of liquid foods and body-fluid,

replaced by the dry, nuggety warmth
of meal in the meal bin,
the soft necklaced fall
of pellets on concrete.

Beyond here there is only Maguire.
The Habitual Truant of Being.
The Economic Migrant of Being.
The Shepherd of Being.

12. Maguire: Wrath of God

Skengs and weed and mummy-cloth. He dreams aloud
forgotten zones, the glaring zones of sacrifice.
Tottenham. Croydon. Colliers Wood. Nine
years have passed, but the gunmetal clouds

are an iron lid they've boiled beneath for centuries.
The riots saw them blow it off completely.
The clatter still resounds: a bin-lid beating
at the edge of town. Here there is only memory-

foam, bubble-wrap shawlies casting about.
Their thousand little bellies drag. Eyes shut, head down
in cradled arms he scans for voices: a drone,
a probe, probe more than drone. An ear. A mouth

floating through the towerblock shebeen,
past silhouettes of men, each one alone
some black, some white. They tunnel
back up neural loanings

to shanties, cabins, radio pips,
Bless, earthen floors with shallow dips
where dogs lap, newspaper tablecloths,
fish scales starring a knife's black handle.

To hitch a ride among the dead concealed.
To flee by way of a beaten path.
To go at night across the muddy gap, spattered
with moon-brimmed hoof-prints, that was the goal.

To feel your way as a cry, retrieve the heart for the shelf
and so establish proper order: As Above,
so Below; Each to his Own; God is Love;
Whatever You're Having Yourself.

Tap. He raises his head from its sweaty halo,
looks over his shoulder. It's so big, this ward,
the floor is levelled against the curvature of the world.
At the foot of his bed smoke two tall beakers of *Red Bull*.

The little tin drum beats in the distance.
One, two, three klicks to the Common
where Bagpuss blinks and yawns,
shifting his sticky haunches in the dust.

13. Beverly Brook

This is how he rolls:
hooded oilskin,
Adidas ski-pants.
Shades. Crocs.

The wheels fold away
into water-tight silos
as the scooter leaves the bank
and turns to face downstream.

Now a holloway grows up,
its matted sky
hung with ribboned plastic.
Tap. Tap. Tap.

Whiskers twitch
in the darkness.
An iris swells.
Pike hang like silent choppers

at the edge of the Zone,
where honey oozes
from the Womble-burrows.
Honey and fire. Look.

There. Floating by on a dirty scallop,
the pinkish quale
of an old cloth cat
that bears the face of Jimi Saville.

14. Anabasis

Rain's rapturous applause: thundergulder
in sizzling dark. Skinnymalinks
of piss-coloured lightning
stoking and strobing the fairway.

I catch him glide, morphing
in the pulse of each scorching
Lichtung: scooter becomes golfcart,
golfcart becomes lawnmower

becomes scooter again, his silhouette black
and vizored, spiked with the stylus
of a tall coroza that earths
the sky, his finger-nails flexed

to long splayed spindly tubers
of whistling electrodes. Again he survives.
Now banana boots. Now bee-beard.
Small dark orbs pop and shudder

in a hyaline jelly around him:
Kirby Crackle, a sackbut of Greek fire.
Attacked from below, he parries
with a volley of orgone

as the last woolly creature flees
if only to succumb: sudden,
sodden, muddy bundle. Terrible,
immobile, decorticated Womble.

15. The Zone

As I roved out across the Zone
my avatar strode before me,
banging her drum and screaming
without a throat. *Boom Boom.*

Into the Zone we went, phantoms
hording at the screen-edge,
a firewall flagged with corpse
and carrion, the bodies of Wombles

picked over by drones. On we stalked.
Homing now for the black rose,
the node, the worrying mass
clapped up on a back-lit light-box.

Close now. Above the watchtower
an image capers and cavorts:
pink and white, heinous, courtly.
Move closer to engage the object.

Which we do, climbing up and in
to what first appears as a ware-
house or ward, then an ICU, a brain,
a cosmic goldfish bowl in which we float,

neuronauts, nanobots,
networked by spatters of black stars,
stars above and stars below, new
and old, stem-end, blossom end,

synapse and prolapse,
negative constellations
spiralling outwards through
a milky soup of spinal fluid.

The cat-headed god yawns his yawn
and picks his teeth
with the sickle moon.
The heart swims up to nestle in my palm.

16. Transfer Window

The pointillist tremor that stimms and shivers next to your ticker
is only your mobile. *Beepity beep.* 'When your enemy's close,
that's how you know it, Daddy'. Yep and so does every bloody
    hologram,
dingbat, duppie and *Fingerbob* abroad tonight, tracking my avatar

marching erratically down the hill. I've got her back though,
and on she goes, so it's only when I hear the scooter's whine
that she stops, half-way down Leopold Road, and jerkily turns
into a digital breeze that rifles in otiose nerdish detail

the stripy blue-and-grey jim-jams she's wearing. A kick-ass,
whoever it was, in Bangalore or mebbe Omsk, that coded these,
    the soft
repeated purl and furl and luminous flicker as the thin material
    stirs,
the answering skittish waver and watery rattle from the bush

of ornamental bamboo, above which the prehensile tip
of the black pointed hood passes by before the whole
thing, the half-cut King, hoves into view, the rim of his cowl
canted back, the moonlight exposing the white wool-knitted

face of what looks like a doll or teddy, doll more than teddy,
more effigy than doll, all lumpen and grubby, much-mended,
Bless, its button-eyes trailing thread, its mouth a smudgy band
of cheap black lippy, what was the nose a puncture-wound welded

with a belt of Evostick. You stand aside. As well you might,
and tap your phone against the one it proffers, the heart
transferring with a chime as he nods, shunts into reverse
and then stops dead, for the little mitten-head has begun to speak.

17. The Head of Oliver Plunkett

'Listen to me. Let me tell you a story. I drifted
over here as a youngster, a lifetime
before your kind did, the runt of a big litter,
falling in with a crowd on night-shift

in the Mentals. That was me for forty
years, man and boy. Wiping people's arses
for a living. Electric shock? Of course
we did! Nobody suffers. It works, doesn't it?

But I do mind sitting in the annexe
once, long past midnight, the dead TV,
the green-on-greener walls slick and shiny,
when up steams the old dumb-waiter and in it

a head. "Here. You're an educated man",
it said (Although I am not.) "What says you
to the way they gathered the hames of my bones
from Downside, Drogheda and Hildesheim,

gathered and raised them up, *sursum corda*
and not to the Lord, no, but carried inside
a shuddersome buzzing yoke, a hellish reliquary
in the shape of a fly, whose head was a black orb,

tool-smooth like a conjuror's, an obsidian crystal
ball, all filled with lights and clockwork things,
with a scorpion's jagged tail, and long black wings
like swords that whirled above it in a circle

and hoisted it up the way a mighty body
might pull a bucket up a scaffolding, so it sways
with its load from side to side but yet holds steady,
up and up, hand over fist, into the motley sky".

It was Oliver Plunkett, the last of the English Martyrs
it says here, his head rotating, the gibbous skin
all mustard and ash, about to explode, like a TV dinner
that's been bubbling in a microwave for all eternity.

This was the head before it had cooled to the boked-
up coconut you see in Drogheda, as it must have been
when snatched by its glib from the fire in Tyburn
and bunged in a sack like a rooster, the way it looked

when moved out from the city in a gallon can, strapped
to the chassis of an artic, banging off the sides, its crowing
lost in the grind of the engine, out through the gates of the city
and on into Surrey where the airbrakes finally hiss and lapse

into the peace of a cobbled courtyard, where fountain
and pear tree water and scent the air, lute and viol
and the head still screeching, carried into cool purple
murmuring shadow, its raging skin balmed and anointed.

That hissing, *Tango*'ed, torn and shrunken dermis
was speaking to me now from its mossy box in a curious
high-faluting accent, a mixture of the North and South, East
and West of Ireland, one minute all spiky consonants and the next

a wheedling, querulous sing-song, one minute a rapid forensic
     mutter
and the next the toothless sough of syllables in rushes
     and all the while
its eyes straying about, bright green and unblinking, lidless eyes,
earless ears, a mouthless mouth that had never ceased to utter:

"At last the helicopter stopped, making no headway,
 but turning very slowly, whether deasil or widdershins
 I cannot remember, for it seemed to me that the land
 itself was rotating and the fly was the still point,

and at that precise moment my bones all called out
to each other, a strange sound, an insect chirrup and chitter
that cut through the pummel and clatter of the rotors,
calling out, begging to be assembled, to be joined at the root

of the brain-stem and the tip of the spinal cord, to be tied
together again at talus and tibia, for my clavicle and scapula
to touch and attach and all of my numbered bones to be wrapped
tightly in a winding sheet and, like a burial at sea, eased

over the gunwale of that infernal engine, so that I might
rise or fall myself, or better remain, a mute white
fixture in the evening sky, bobbin or spool that cannot
unbind, chrysalis pinned to the velvet board of night".

Much else it told me, how the pilot sat impassively
against the sky, a painted effigy, as the bones began
to descend, London brooding below them, an early sun
striking fire off dome and steeple, the intricate city

stretching to the horizon, and running through it the Thames
shining and transparent, a snail's evaporating glister, the loop
around the Dog's peninsula dangling like the cabled noose
that hangs from the gibbet's blanched and lichened arm.

And as they had thronged to see him suffer at Tyburn Cross,
so now a crowd was waiting on the Common, their faces
upturned, though when the chopper settled and the blades ceased
in their din, becoming visible again, we heard not the raucous

jeers and blather of the mob, but rather a great shared
sigh, the kind that exhales itself in the silence back of
a ding-dong, a post-everything whisper, the kind that occurs
when the gallows speech packs in, the breathless gap after death-

rattle, drum batter, thunder-storm, the aftermath of the dum-
dum that was not a dummy, of the blast inside the citadel,
it's in that vested weight, that pressure-drop, that tumult
you hear voices disinter themselves, the dead voices are the sum

of that change, you get me, that sudden feinted buckle
is where they hail from, not some gross throat
fleshing quickly along neck bones, not the woven,
sleeving cordage, but the waft of the wind thrapple,

pure sound brought out of itself, a mouthless whistle,
not some vegetal glottis flexing at its centre of its pentacle,
not the uvula's carnal bleb, but a sine wave, imperceptible
tremble of the middle air, as the water table

in a tumbler on a table trembles long after the column
of armour passes, as the Geiger counter garrulously ticks
in the middle of the rainy swaying pine plantation, as
the lanyard's ghost still taps against the logged flagpole's absence.

18. Tronies

The voice stopped and the sock-puppet fizzog began to waver
    and roil,
the thin black line of the mouth was a ripple that stilled,
    like a wavelength
on a monitor above a gurney, and then it was gone, replaced
    by a tense
mugshot, an umber *tronie*, the face of an old man, his bald,
    soft-boiled,

sonorous skull failed and fungal, but stern with it, as if this
    were one
accustomed to power, as if Bellini's fanatical hard-faced Doge
had been disencumbered of *corno* and acorn-buttoned robes,
to be laid out instead upon a dirty canvas stretcher. Only then
    he became

a pope or a cardinal, his mobility-bike a cube of glass and steel,
and I caught a whiff of shit and kitchens as the face drained
    slowly
into the maw of its own scream, was forced to look away
    to the gnarly
spotted hands that gripped the handles of the machine, then
    to see

the crinkled plastic sheath that covered his slender little willy,
    a sheath welling
up with a toffee-coloured syrup, as my gaze fell down the
    hairless pins,
puffy at the knees, the yellow shanks, towards a pair of
    tigerfeet slippers, that turned
as I stared into winklepickers, buffed and shining, their laces
    tying themselves,

while my eye crawled up the edge of the straight razored crease in
    his trousers,
black or dark blue, a kind of teddyboy look but sober with it, one
    pocket
crammed with a meaty left hook, sweeping back a two-button
    jacket,
the other held out, pinkie ring, burning snout, *JPS Black* or
    Gallagher's

Green, the racing form beneath his arm, a clean white shirt open
    at the neck,
a pompadour, the bluest eyes, I have never seen eyes so blue, *bless*,
    looking up
at the stars where a landing light was winking to its private pad,
    eyes that shut
and opened inside my own eyes, *bless*, the helicopter aligning
    itself, dipping back

behind a discreetly fortified fence, so the sound of the hurdling
    rotors
was muffled, then cancelled, *bless*, and I could hear the quiver
    of trees, the dull
St Mary's carillon, and what seemed to be sighs, cries,
    the sleepy whistle
of a bird as my own mouth opened, mouthing words
    that his mouth spoke.

19. The Gambrel

'Spring is a bit of an issue this year,
the sticky tissues of the buds,
the budding leaves, the solstice,
the shenanigans

up on the limestone plateau,
where Tomsk patrols
the willow grove,
all slabbered in woad

and what-have-you,
with his arse painted blue,
his sleeve tattoos,
his shaky grasp of personal grooming.

Out of his skull on DMT,
he keeps smelling roses
where there are none. Roses. Rosewater.
Some kind of gorgeous ointment.

The mobile in his hand
shining like an ear of corn, his fur
combed out into little red points.
He is hunting for Uncle Bulgaria.

Hunting down the ageing King,
Alpha of the primal horde
of Wombles. Hogger of the lady Wombles.
Even the Moomins want him dead,

hung like a ham from a gambrel,
strung up like a ham or a hock
while the lads draw lots
for his tartan cope, his tartan tocque.'

20. Ambush

Even the Common
wants him dead.
Even the Common
knows Maguire
is tatie bread.

4.00 am.

The image on my tablet
swims and drifts again,
the clouds of the sky
pass over, fading
to half-remembered shades.

Coal pitch.
Whale bone.

Save only for
the payload of rose
limping slowly
down the screen.

A sacred heart.
A body part.
A giveaway glow
of mammal heat.

Sheen more than glow.
Star more than sheen.

This image must be being streamed
from the chopper, whose drear,
monotonous chuckle
I can just about catch
from somewhere along the Ridgeway.

Heart.
Mouth.

Four shades.
Four braves.

Two by two
they move as one.
I watch his rosy node bloom
and fail. *Puff.* I watch it go out.

21. Kenosis

I opened my mouth in a dream
and in the real I closed it.
What happened in between?

Daddy, can't you see I'm burning?

The inflatable pig is toast.
I won it at the fete.
I shot it in the head, like Axl Rose.

Daddy, can't you see I'm burning?

The pig was a poem, it squeaked
against my cortex
as we both began to peak.

Daddy can't you see I'm burning?

I did it humanly. Far as I know.
I did it in the conservatory.
I was listening to Marti Pellow.

Daddy can't you see I'm burning?

I hear the rotors overhead.
My face breaks out in larval tears.
I touch the wizened plastic shreds.

Daddy, can't you see I'm burning?

Soon you'll see the heavens shoal.
The wizened plastic shreds I touch.
My dog has got no nose.

Daddy, can't you see I'm burning?

22. The Heart

Apropos of nothing, the corroded red datum
silted upright on the moonlit seabed
of your brain, after over half a lifetime,
began to transmit a sequence of primes.

Though seemingly aimed at Jupiter's
gammy peeper, they are picked up
by the close-fitting black beanie
you had taken to wearing in bed.

Bless. It was wired to an ancient Tom-Tom
on which a jewelled tumour shook
and tremored, stuttering out a location
on the horizon of your hippocampus.

Bingo. You grabbed the *Adventure Kit*:
the black-handled blade, the torch, the camera,
swam out of the house of sleep
and pushed straight up the cranial pathway

of a lamp post, till a current caught you,
routing you right through the gateway
to the Common. First you orbit, then descend,
arms out-stretched, stripy pyjama legs belling,

to where your own body lies prostrate inside
the circular, open-air ruin. You are asleep.
Neural stars glint in the murk.
Beside you the heart, the numbered bones.

23. Moominbeckett

I

It feels like it's about to snow, that foreboding
sense of weight and silence, a signal from the sky-
docked cloud. At the tower. I slip my phone
from my breast to snap her in her clamber

up the rigging, *bless*, but it's frozen in selfie mode,
the image magnified fish-eye style so I find
myself peering deep into my own left nostril,
where a thing is shining out, a crystalline

structure sinking slowly down, projected upon it
a long but bulbous face, snout more than face,
conk more than snout, hippo-like, very white,
all parched and scrotal, no mouth at all. The gull-blue

eyes are deeply scored with infinite lines,
there are lines across the staring brow, lines piled
high to the pointed ears and between them
a quartz anemone that tinkles, chimes.
                                    Then a low voice:

II

'Nothing moves
in my veins out here
and nothing ever will,

crystal and stone
and coral and bone
are all that is real,

all that is cold
is all that abides
let silica stone

crystal and bone
shine out of your soul
let your soul be content

with cloud and stone
so the polar light
shines out of your eye

your heart become home
to the spirit-bone
the seal

the Groke
the scop
the skua

the thing
that inhabits
the wintery zone

in the lee
of a ruined dome
or rotunda

scrolling light
now black
now white

eternal diurnal
hyperborean temple no
entrance no exit

its roof cut away
at an angle revealing
a humanoid form

all succour and calm
beside him his bones
disassembled replenished

exposed to the sky
they sing they chirp
they bless they hiccup

totally smooth
totally clean
scoured and borne

by solar winds
or carried in a solar boat
above remote primordial oceans.

III

The stars above
and the rock below
the dome holds steady

in the snow
the drifts of snow
that cloud the rock

the wind of grit
that sands the bones
beside the creature

incredibly old
cryogenically frozen
lying in profile

the muzzle set
the brow unlined
shining out

immaculate
the delicate ear
its plug of fur

the wattled neck
its jugular
one visible eye

cast up to heaven
blue inhumed
begging

the question
what place is this
what zone what region?

IV

The fur on his flank
is rising subsiding
each easeful breath

an aeon
an instant
in synch with

controlling
light and cold
sudden strobe

or slow oscillation
the landscape goes
from white to grey

the dome
the snow
the rock the bones

from white to grey
then grey to black
the sky

the cloud
the eye
the fur

from freezing point
to fifty below
the chest

the arms
ensleeved in sheets
then back again

but rarely higher
certainly never
exceeding zero.

V

You pick up each sigh
such is the silence
a scatter of molars

a pattern of knuckles
the sky above is
inside out

scene cordoned off
ceremonial site
the counter-life

of bone and snow
of stars arrayed
beneath the dome

that's broken open
to a sun
of silicon

a coral eye
the snow is rising
to the sky

your dad is dead
in negative
is constellate

of star and bone
is tantamount
to light in eye

of eye and light
a concentrate
a bone-bright crystal

on your lash
weighed assayed
and not found wanting.

24. Trinity

Midnight. I'm at the watchtower,
its darkened hutch,
a hatchery beneath
the roof's blunt dovecote,

nicked and deckled at the eaves,
as if comprised of leaves
and not Kevlar, as if
we didn't know the going rate

for ivory and iron ore,
for nickel and coal...
Everything great
stands in the storm, you say,

but I incline to stillness,
like this mist that clings
to bark and bole
when no wind blows.

I squeeze inside the chute
that slowly draws me up,
as if by peristalsis, a last dry heave
easing me onto the slatted deck.

Bless. Three blue birds in the silver tree:
Mary, Mungo and *Midge.*
Sentinels of the upper air.
Beneath their gaze I'll go to sleep.

25. The Slide

I was thinking to hoist
my mobile up to the glare
in two hands like a host.
I was hoping to catch her.

I was at the top of the slide.
I saw Daddy's new phone,
and thought take a picture of me,
send it on to mummy.

But when I did she was gone.
There was no-one there.
An empty screen.
But for the watchtower.

I was somewhere else: flying
between the sky and the earth
for a second, feeling like a small dry
Moomin sleeping through the winter.

Moving. Just in time to feel,
as I stepped towards the chute,
the soft blow to my knees that
bundled us backwards, her and me,

me and him, like the silly horse
in a pantomime, bless,
falling down on the wet grass.
That's when you rang us.

26. Southfields Look-Out

Let's not, just yet, return to life
down the lookout's knotty ladder,
let's stay up here a little while,
to watch the light of what might be stars
quiver in the slow dissolve
of London's spectacular caul.

The wind carries up the birds that sound
like droids or a car-alarm; and now
the reversing-bin-lorry-bird; and soon,
(no more than a second or two)
an ambulance howl for all the world
like the one for which we weren't prepared:

our daughter's, heard first it seems,
only an instant since; though that song,
that hungry, headlong human cry,
cracked the face of my mobile phone
eight years ago, long before this back-lit dawn
scrolled up its grey-blue sonogram.

Daylight clouds are product-placed,
skilfully arranged, draped
in careful layers that, like dry-ice,
come to impersonate
white wool for our eyes: finials, fishtails,
or the belly of the great ghost-whale

that has kept us lately in its lours,
fast inside its worldly smile,
and set me adrift in the early hours
through blurry chambers, virtually
unconscious, its smoke and mirrors
that pass through and through us.

It will shroud us again. Meanwhile
her voice ventriloquized outstrips
caul, birds, clouds, whale,
and we have begun to dehisce
at last, slipping through the shells
we grew in the bad days, held

up here beneath the stars
to watch the dawn and hear the siren wail,
carried up as if on a plume of hard
water, aloft on the same shrill
wind, the same keen air, that kept our
old dears up all night, and blew them clear.

27. The Mobility Vehicle

In the spiritual gloom of a lock-up,
a little electric motor snores,
and will run a short while longer
on juice they hack from the Big Six.

They have prepared it, gilded the wheels
and handles with gold: the foil from Easter eggs
and blister packs; crushed stamens; anthers.
As the horns and hooves of the sacrifice
were gilded, and garlanded with flowers.

At dawn the youngest leads it outside
to expose it on the concrete apron,
watching the little girl
precisely anoint the customary places:
an axle's oily oxter, the steering column's vertebrae.

Patrick's Day. The pipes. The pipes. A burst
on the tinny tin drum
is followed by a directional scream
that shatters the headlight and mirrors,
the screen of every last device in Wimbledon.

Now they wait for the earliest scavenger:
me. I circle and sit, circle again,
then warily approach, my two ears flush
with the sides of my skull,
glad to have a part to play,
but showing respect, taking only my due.

28. English Martyrs

Look. A Chinook, hammock slung between two grey derricks,
  very low,
hanging fire, then angling heavily down and away, as if the tower
  at the tail
had been pinched between a fastidious thumb and forefinger,
  escorted out
of this summer day like the pesky mouse in yestermorning's *Tom
  and Jerry*.

Silence. Now look. Two furls of smoke from our barbecue pit
  weave up
in a helix, an impermanent spiralling twister, a couple of
  copulating serpents,
each bound about the other, *bless*, rasping and slithery, wriggly
  and sibilant,
a snookered caduceus thrashing inside the voice box of the
  Common, the voice

box, the black box, the glory and priest-hole. Echo-socket. Yokey-
  buzzer.
An empty set, a clearing house, a vernal emission, combined and
  uneven.
A wildflower's calyx humming with hexes and pesters, coos and
  prustens,
woofs, tweets and geckers. A bee-mouth-grille. A little pink or
  blue kazoo.

A semi-conducting portal for pant-hoots, *bless*, like the bouncy
  pontoon
crossing Beverley Brook, where the martyred voices blow in
  colloquy
and counterpoint, Fisher and More, coughing in bole and leaf-
  blower, ingle-
nook and keyhole, chanting in tongue and groove, cobweb and
  cooling tower.

Their gobbledygook is grafted onto particle and polymer, root
    and radial.
It spreads by contagion, by capillary suasion, a legion, a lurgy,
    the legbone
connected to the collarbone, the collarbone connected to
    the nose-flute.
Pepsi & Shirlie, Kelso Cochrane, Chief Long Wolf, *Cannon & Ball*.

Starting to seethe now, bubbling down in the lees of the whale like
    a full English
breakfast, crooning from the zeros, the binary codes, the whale
    bone connected to
the genome, the genome connected to the Overton window,
    Sarah Namala, Robert Emmett.
Billing and cooing from the dry, tidemarked throats of porcelain
    cisterns in padlocked

municipal lavs, *bless*, keening through the twin little colons in
    Bazalgette's
manholes, Richard Gwyn, David Lewis, the backbone connected
    to the cash flow,
the cash flow connected to the drop zone, the neurone connected
    to the ink stone.
Stirring in the lift-shafts and the windlasses of the tower blocks,
    stained white cliffs where

the gannets preen, smooth breasts bedabbled with ketchup,
    Cuthbert Howlett,
Alice Samuel, calling through the star-crossed panes of benefit
    hostels
etch-a-sketched with forgotten initials, Kevin Gately,
    Agnes Waterhouse,
breathing from the toothless gobs of postboxes, from the kissers
    of vape sticks.

Hissing from the unshackled earbud of a drowsy boy on an
    otherwise empty
nightbus, *bless*, or trickling from the narrow neck of a defrocked
    sugar sachet

in the tea room of HMP Wandsworth, the tea room that was
   once the gallows:
the Stratton Brothers, William Joyce, *Little & Large*, the hip bone
connected to the peep-hole, the allophone connected to
   the yongy-bongy-bo,

Sapphire & Steel, *bless*, Naomi Hersi, *bless*, Hammett and Brine,
   bless,
Hinge & Bracket, gah, the mouth-hole connected to the asshole,
   the asshole
that's grassing to a footpatrol, the footpatrol that's searching for
   the old mole.

Bland and Frankesh, *bless*, Bodie & Doyle, ach, Larkin and
   O'Brien, *bless*.
Mewling in the grim flues of kebab shops, in the cindery exhaust
   pipes
of delivery mopeds, the trombone connected to the wig-wam,
   the ding-dong
connected to the bunga-bunga. Altab Ali. Blair Peach. Edward
   Jakubowsky.

And all those you couldn't put a name to, never ever put a name
   to:
Janet & John, let's say; *Meg & Mog*, let's say; *Bill & Ben*, let's say.
Sooty & Sweep, let's say; *Pinky & Perky*, let's say; *Crystal Tips
   & Alastair.*
Uncle Bulgaria, let's say. Mistah Kurtz, let's say. John Maguire,
   let's say.
Bless.

Whispering from the gaps between the dry, dusty lips of two
   large bags
of sawdust, Sacha Murphy, Joe Meek, two full-bellied torsos
   dragged to the jail
in Horsemongers Street in 1802, Edward Despard, Robert Drury,
   Cherry Groce,
bless, lugged to the jail and into its courtyard, Ball and Tyler,

Tyler and Straw,
the frayed chapped lips around their mouths, the dust bone
connected to the blood
bone, the blood bone connected to the neck bone, the neck
bone connected
to the axe bone, *bless*, brought into the smoggy courtyard and
set beside the block,
Dipsy and LaLa, the Demdikes and the Chattoxes, the daddy
bone and the

mummy bone, the daughter bone, Joan, Margaret and
Philippa Flowers, *bless*,
faint breath in the crumbling mouths, the dry mouths of a
couple of sacks
of sawdust, *bless*, breathless, *bless*, Alan Turing, Mark Fisher, a
blue cloud
in the fasting holes, Oliver Plunkett, Roger Casement, the
faintest of whispers

stirring the dust, the sawdust and the bone dust, the smoke
dust and the coal
breath, the lip bone and the dirt song, the song dust and the
heart bone, the ash
bone and *Boney M*, a fish bone, a foul bone, the heart's mouth,
the bone dream,
the spirit bone, the occult zone, the throat bone,
the dust breath, a bone song.

Two Rivers Press has been publishing in and about Reading
since 1994. Founded by the artist Peter Hay (1951–2003),
the press continues to delight readers, local and further afield,
with its varied list of individually designed,
thought-provoking books.